LIVING
GIFTED

52 Tips to Survive and Thrive in Giftedland

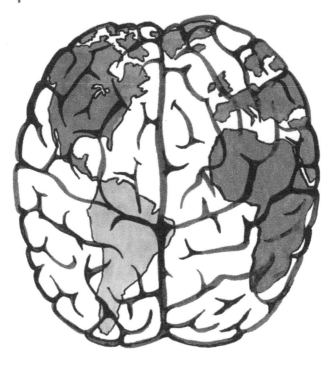

LISA VAN GEMERT M.Ed.T.

Published by Gifted Guru Publishing

©2019 Gifted Guru Publishing

Printed in the United States of America.

ISBN 9781796644166

Book cover design by Okomota

For Abigail Paige

As soon as I saw you,

I knew an adventure was going to happen.

– Winnie-the-Pooh

Table of Contents

Preface

About a year ago I attended a seminar on writing, and one of the presenters, Betsy Allen-Manning, talked about the process of writing a tip book. A tip book, she explained, was a small volume with your best ideas you could share to improve someone's experience in an area in which you had expertise.

She had us do a little brainstorming there that night, and while many around the table were thinking, I was busy writing. The ideas flew faster than my pen could write them down.

What if I could share 52 tips with teens and adults about navigating this world of giftedness? What if I could have a minute or so to share an idea that has helped me? What if...

I saw her two days later at another event, and I already had an outline. I couldn't do anything else until all of these ideas had been written down.

This slim volume you are reading now is the result of that night. It took months of research and drafting after the initial ideas flew, and it is here now. I hope that they help you as they have helped me.

- Lisa Van Gemert, January 15, 2019

Section I:

Motivating the Gifted Brain

Tip #1
Motivation is Mission Critical

Motivation is a word that gets thrown around a lot, so what does it mean?

Motivation means the tendencies you possess that make it possible to reach your goals.

Guess whose job it is to motivate you? If you guessed it's your job, you're right.

Research shows that three things are necessary for us to feel internal motivation (motivation that comes from inside of us, rather than because we're getting a reward or punishment).

We need to feel:

- Autonomy: We have some control over what we're doing

- Mastery: We're learning new skills, that it's not the same ol' thing

- Purpose: Our work matters for more than a grade or profit

Motivation will almost always beat mere talent.
                                    – Norman Ralph Augustine

Which of these motivation skills do you have?

Check if it describes you!

☒ Achievement drive: I continually strive to do excellent work, even if no one is forcing me.

__ Initiative: I am ready to act on opportunities that present themselves to me. I try things and take risks.

☒ Optimism: I persist in my goals and don't get overly discouraged by obstacles and setbacks.

Decide which of the three you will work on and write it here:

Initiative

If you're interested in learning more about this, read Dan Pink's book *Drive: The Surprising Truth About What Motivates Us.*

All of his books are terrific, and this one is my favorite book on motivation.

Tip #2
Learn How to Set Both Broad And Narrow Goals

Having a big goal increases motivation. When you know that the task you're doing is moving you toward that goal, it helps you keep working even when the going gets tough.

At the same time, gifted people often change those big goals quite often, and you can end up feeling like you never achieve anything because your target keeps moving.

The solution? Make sure that you set some narrower goals in addition to your big goals.

Narrow goals give you the opportunity to feel a sense of accomplishment and progress, even if your broad goals are a moving target.

A broad goal would be to become a doctor.

A narrow goal would be to get CPR certified. Even if you change your mind about becoming a doctor, you still have accomplished something useful to you (and others).

Perseverance is not a long race; it is many short races one after the other.

- Walter Elliot

Write down one broad goal you have right now.

Play college football

Think of two narrow goals that you could also set for yourself
that would give you a skill you will have for a long time:

1. _Be a team captain_

2. _~~Bb~~ Be a highschool_

Tip #3
Use the Power of Dopamine

Your brain is a chemistry factory, and one of those chemicals, a neurotransmitter called dopamine, has the power to help you develop your internal motivation.

You get a little release of dopamine every time any one of these things happens:

- You make a guess

- Your guess is correct

- You think you might get a prize, a gift, or a reward

- You actually do get a prize, a gift you like, or a reward

- You feel good about accomplishing something

- You help someone

- You thought something was going to go wrong, but it ended up okay

- You see someone you like

You can get dopamine through harmful ways as well, like addictions, but the most powerful use of dopamine in your life is to practice recognizing it when it comes and using that understanding to help you stay motivated.

Dopamine Data

For a week, keep track of all of the times you feel that surge of dopamine. As you do this, you will become more proficient at knowing what makes your brain happy. Evaluate if the source is good for you in the long run, or if you are being misled by dopamine into habits that aren't helpful.

This week I felt dopamine surges when I:

_____

_____

_____

_____

_____

_____

_____

_____

Tip #4
Add a Layer of Service

Gifted people often have what is called "early moral concern." That's a fancy way of saying that they care more deeply at younger ages for other people.

When you feel your motivation waning, you can leverage that early moral concern by making the task less about you and more about others.

For instance, if you have a homework assignment with 35 problems, ask your parents if they'll donate five cents to a charity you care about for every problem you do correctly and thoroughly.

If you have chores you just can't seem to get the mental energy to engage in, make yourself a deal that when the chore is done well, you will send a text message to someone who you know has been having a hard time or you will play fetch with your dog for five minutes.

It seems counterintuitive perhaps, but focusing on someone other than yourself can help you find the motivation for even your least favorite tasks.

Add a Layer

What's a cause you care about?

_____

What's one way you could connect that to work you have to do, like chores, homework, or other tasks?

_____

What's the first step you would need to make that happen?

_____

Schedule that step.

Tip #5
Time Your Task

Do you ever put off a task for a long time, dreading even the thought of it, only to find that it didn't take as long as you thought it would? Maybe it wasn't nearly as bad as you thought it would be, either.

Sometimes we spend more time and mental energy procrastinating doing our work than we would have spent just doing the work.

Consider timing the tasks that you often put off or dread. For instance, cleaning out your backpack may be something that makes you feel like all of your energy just got sucked out of the bottom of your foot, but when you actually time it, you may find that it only takes you five minutes.

Is it really worth all of that anguish for a five-minute task? You don't have to be gifted to realize that makes no sense.

As soon as you feel yourself resisting a task, set a time for how long you think it will take and race yourself a little. Two things will happen: you will likely find that it wasn't as bad as you feared, and if you beat your guessed time, you'll get a shot of dopamine for a bonus!

Time Your Tasks!

In the table below, list tasks you find yourself dreading or putting off doing. Make a guess as to how much time the task takes. The next time the task comes up, time yourself. How long did it really take? If it took longer than you thought, you still have valuable information. You now know how long it takes and can plan in the future.

TASK	GUESSED TIME	ACTUAL TIME	DIFFERENCE

Tip #6
Motivation Can Be Overrated

There's a lot of talk about finding your passion and doing passion projects and focusing on doing what you love. Here's a big secret: most people don't get to do what they like all of the time. Most people doing dishes aren't ecstatic. Most people taking out the trash could think of something else they'd rather be doing.

Guess what most people have in common who do get to do what they like all or most of the time?

They spent a lot of time doing things they didn't particularly enjoy. They worked long and hard at things first (and they probably still do).

You don't need to feel overjoyed and excited about every task, project, and assignment that comes your way.

Don't be one of those short-sighted people who think, "I don't see why I should have to (fill-in-the-blank). I don't like doing that."

That's what immature people think. Grow up and realize that it's not just about what you want to do. It's about what needs to be done. If you find yourself falling into that trap, remind yourself that you're behaving in an immature way and recalibrate your thinking.

What's something that you don't really like doing but you know needs to be done?

_____

What's something bad that would or could happen if that thing were not done?

_____

What is something other people don't like doing but that you don't mind doing?

_____

How much does this statement describe you?

I frequently complain about or resist tasks I don't like to do.

Not at all like me.

Somewhat like me.

Very much like me.

If that statement is very much like you, set a goal for yourself to make it less like you.

Tip #7
Develop Your
Internal Locus of Control

Do you believe you control your own destiny? Do you believe that you can impact your life significantly through your action (or inaction)?

Psychologist Julian Rotter proposed that people's idea of the level of control they had over their own lives had a strong and direct impact on happiness.

This is called an "internal locus of control" and the more you have, the better off you are.

It is not an either/or situation. We all have a stronger internal locus of control in some areas than others.

The opposite of internal locus of control is external locus of control. This is when you feel like other people are responsible for your success and happiness. You feel that you are at the mercy of the actions of others.

Sometimes we're not in full control, but we have partial control.

Set your intention to recognize all the ways in which you *are* in control, rather than focusing on the ways in which you aren't.

Circle AGREE or DISAGREE
with the following statements:

1. A lot of the time I feel that I'm not really in control of my life and what happens to me.

    AGREE   DISAGREE

2. I believe that if I study effectively for a test, I have the ability to do well.

    AGREE   DISAGREE

3. I think that no matter what people do, their destiny is set for them.

    AGREE   DISAGREE

4. I don't think that most success is about luck or what you're born with. I think it's more about how hard you work.

    AGREE   DISAGREE

5. Individuals have very little power or influence over the events in the world and even their own lives.

    AGREE   DISAGREE

KEY: If you agreed with questions 2 & 4, you are on the path to a strong internal locus of control.

Tip #8
Gratitude Fuels Motivation

Grateful people are usually motivated people.

A lack of motivation can be a sign of a lack of appreciation for what you've been given, of the advantages you have.

You may not think of yourself as having a lot of advantages, but if you're reading this, you already have a huge advantage over millions of people: you can read.

When you realize how lucky you are to have what you have, it's easier to feel motivated to use the talents and gifts you've been given to grow yourself or to help others.

If you find yourself feeling unmotivated or less motivated than you usually do, focus on gratitude for awhile. Recognize the people who have helped you and continue to help you. Acknowledge the skills you've been taught. Consider all of your ancestors who lived before so many of the miracles we take for granted every day and how happy they would be to know that you have all that you have.

Your life is as wonderful as it is because other people have made it possible.

Never forget that, nor forget them.

Here's an acrostic of the word GRATITUDE.

Next to each letter, write something you are grateful for that starts with that letter.

G _____

R _____

A _____

T _____

I _____

T _____

U _____

D _____

E _____

Tip #9

Avoiding Seeking Rewards For Deep Thinking And Precious Products

Rewards work for low-level tasks. They backfire when tasks are complicated or full of meaning.

It's fine to set reward schedules up for yourself to help you gain the motivation you need to get boring, repetitive tasks done like filling out forms or folding laundry.

It's essential, though, that you avoid rewarding yourself or seeking or expecting reward for deeper tasks like learning or helping. Think of them less as tasks and more as opportunities.

If you seek rewards for those kinds of things, you will do less well on the task, you will not enjoy it as much, you will lose sight of its real value to you, and you will become a more shallow person than you were meant to be.

If you find yourself asking, "What do I get if I do it?," you are on the wrong mental path. Make a course correction. Stop yourself and think, "What is the value of this task in the long run, either for me or for others?"

For every opportunity listed below, think of a benefit that could be gained by doing it well and without whining. Remember that the benefit may be long term, so don't be fooled into thinking it's just about what you can get right now. Very few important things reveal their true value in the moment. Most benefits take time to unfurl.

TASK	BENEFIT
homework	
making your bed	
not making a rude comment	
being kind to a rude person	
sharing something you really wanted	
listening politely	
visiting someone you don't really like that much	
playing a game that's not your favorite	

Tip #10
Fuel Your Motivation with Story

The fundamental basis of motivation is story – your story. What do you really think you are on this Earth to do? How is what you are doing right here, right now part of that mission?

I have a friend named Leland Melvin who is a real, live astronaut. He's flown on the space shuttle not once, but twice. He's been to the International Space Station. He's the real deal.

Leland no longer flies in space, but he knows that he is still on a mission – a mission to help students learn the science and math they need to prepare themselves for their own adventures in our world and beyond. He spends a lot of his work effort focused on helping others achieve the goals he has had the opportunity to live.

Leland's story is the rocket fuel of his motivation. He doesn't waste time worrying about how every little thing helps him. His story is more broad than himself.

What's your story?

What are you here to do, and how can you connect what you're being asked to do right now to that story? Your story will likely change over time, and that's fine. What's important is that you have one. You're not an astronaut, but you're definitely on a mission.

What's Your Story Right Now?

_____

_____

_____

_____

_____

Photo Credit: NASA

This is Leland's official NASA photo. He snuck the dogs in to NASA to get them in the picture! Want to get to know Leland and his story better? Read his book *Chasing Space: An Astronaut's Story of Grit, Grace, and Second Chances.*

Section II:

Brain Health for Great Brains

Tip #11
Guard Your Sleep As You Would A Precious Jewel

Gifted people often have issues with sleep. Sometimes we struggle to fall asleep, and sometimes we struggle to get back to sleep when we wake up in the middle of the night.

This makes sense because sleep is a busy time for the brain. It's trying to clean up everything that happened during the day that made a brain mess so that it can be ready for the next day.

Just like other aspects of brain function, when you've got a busy brain, it's going to work differently than a typical brain. If you feel your brain spinning in the night, try to avoid feeling stressed about it. The stress you feel doesn't serve you.

Instead of lying there thinking, "I'm going to be so tired in the morning" and other similar thoughts, remind yourself that it's normal to have trouble sleeping sometimes.

At the same time, avoid undermining your sleep by staying up super late on weekends, using devices with blue light in the evening, telling yourself you only need five hours of sleep, and other unhealthy habits.

Never brag about being too busy to sleep. It doesn't mean you're important; it means you don't understand some pretty simple science.

Read this article on sleep: bit.ly/gifted-sleep

What are three things you can do to improve your sleep habits? Write them down, try them for two weeks, and then come back and reflect on what worked and what didn't.

1. _____

2. _____

3. _____

Two weeks later....what happened?

_____

_____

_____

_____

Tip #12
Don't Get Hijacked by Your Screen

Technology is great. It really is. It is also a potential problem. Too many people have allowed virtual reality to become their reality. The research is still being done, but we know that screens use (some would say hijack) the rewards system in the brain.

The same system that makes you happy when people give you likes and comments creates anxiety when you don't get them. The same system that makes you glad to see a text from a friend creates anxiety when you know you have a notification and can't check it or don't have access to your phone.

The constant distractions may be making it harder for you to focus, even when you want to.

The issues go on and on, and it's not your fault. Companies that make games and apps know just how to create a need on your part to engage with their product. Interested in learning more? Read this article about how companies are trying to hack your brain on purpose http://bit.ly/screen-hacking.

Be smart about screens. Make them your servant, not the other way around.

Answer these questions honestly:

1. Would other people in my life say that I am preoccupied or obsessed with video games/devices?

   Yes   Maybe   No

2. Do I feel stressed or anxious when I can't play video games or be on my phone?

   Yes   Sometimes   Rarely   Never

3. Have I lost interest in other hobbies or things I used to like to do and really just want to play on a screen?

   Yes   No

4. Have I ever lied about how much I play to my parents or others?

   Yes   No

5. Have I missed out on an opportunity or made someone upset that I wouldn't spend time with them because I would rather be playing a game?

   Yes   No

Then, complete this screen audit for a week and see how much time you're really spending http://bit.ly/screen-audit.

Tip #13
Acquire Another Language

Knowing a second language is a bonanza to the brain. Here are just a few benefits that come to people who speak more than one language:

- They know their own language better. I never really understood the subjunctive in English until I learned about it in Spanish class. If you don't know what I mean by "subjunctive," then I kind of proved my point.

- They can handle noisy environments better. If you are bilingual, it's easier for you to tune out noise you don't want to pay attention to. That's a huge benefit if you're someone who is distracted by buzzing fluorescent lights.

- They're more creative. When we understand things through the lens of different languages, it appears to make us more creative in our thinking in general.

- They protect their brains by exercising them. It turns out that exercising your brain by running more than one language program in it is good for it. Just like your heart, your brain functions well with a little exercise.

- They have better executive functioning skills. You know, so you don't just *do* your homework – you actually turn it in.

If you want to build your brain, another language is the perfect place to start.

Read more about the benefits of learning another language, as well as get ideas for choosing a language to learn at http://bit.ly/brain-language.

Match the language facts below to see how much you already know about the languages of the world by the numbers!

Number of languages in the world	Approximately 1,000
Number of official languages of the United Nations	Approximately 800
Number of languages spoken in Papua, New Guinea	74
Number of letters in longest alphabet in the world (Cambodian)	More than 6,000
Number of languages spoken on the continent of Africa	6

Answers: Languages in world: 6,000; UN languages: 6; Languages in Papua, New Guinea: 800; Letters in longest alphabet: 74; Languages in Africa: 1,000.

Tip #14
Quiz Yourself If No One Else Will

Researchers at Washington University in St. Louis have learned something really interesting about learning: the importance of quizzes. It turns out that the brain pays a lot of attention when it thinks it's going to be tested.

Frequent quizzing is more effective than some more common study tactics like highlighting, re-reading, looking over notes, etc.

If you want to learn material well, consider quizzing yourself. You can do it old school with simple flashcards, or you can use an online quiz platform to create quizzes.

Keep in mind that what seems to work best is something called "interleaving," meaning that it's helpful to keep studying material from the whole year, not just what you're learning right now.

Here's an example: let's say you're studying historical facts. Rather than just quizzing the facts from the current chapter you're studying, you would also quiz yourself on the facts you've learned all year (or maybe even years before). Even after the teacher has moved on from the Civil War, you will keep quizzing yourself on it.

Try using a grid like this to help you make sure that you're quizzing yourself on a wide variety of material, keeping it all fresh in your mind.

LAST WEEK	WAY BACK	MOST RECENT	LAST WEEK
TWO WEEKS AGO	MOST RECENT	WAY BACK	TWO WEEKS AGO
LAST WEEK	TWO WEEKS AGO	MOST RECENT	WAY BACK

When you're setting up your quiz, make sure to include lots of different types of questions and problems. Challenge yourself, and it will pay off in the end.

Tip #15
Challenge Your Brain

When you have an efficient brain, it can take more effort to challenge it, but that challenge is absolutely necessary. Why?

It is absolutely essential that you avoid the dreaded *Lazy Brain Syndrome.* Lazy Brain Syndrome is a common condition among the gifted that occurs when we get too used to things coming easily to us. We just go with the flow of whatever challenge comes our way.

Sounds great, doesn't it? Except it's not.

The reason it's not is that when you are too *laissez-faire* (useful French term that means "letting things just take their own course") about how hard your brain is working, you can become overwhelmed too easily when a challenge arises. It's like a boulder in the middle of your gently flowing river, and it can capsize your canoe.

Seek challenge for your brain by learning a language (as mentioned in Tip #13), working on something that doesn't come naturally easy to you, learning a musical instrument, memorizing useful/interesting facts, etc.

Constant challenge keeps Lazy Brain Syndrome away.

Bonus: you always have something to think about when there's too little going on to hold your interest.

Choose one (or more) of the challenges below to protect yourself against Lazy Brain Syndrome.

✓ Learn to count to 100 in three languages.

✓ Memorize the first 100 digits of π.

✓ Memorize the Periodic Table of the elements.

✓ Learn all of the words to five patriotic songs or hymns or other songs you wish you knew.

✓ Think of a problem facing the world and develop a plan for solving it.

✓ Memorize poetry. Read more about what I think about that at: http://bit.ly/gg-poetry.

✓ Write a book. Hey! You could write a tip book like this one!

✓ Learn calligraphy or brush writing.

✓ Learn a martial art or yoga.

✓ Learn chess or another strategy game.

✓ Learn to draw a map of the world. (I'm working on this right now using a book by Kristin Draeger called *Draw the World*.)

Tip #16
Improve Your Imagination

Imagination is as important to the gifted brain as knowledge and reasoning. The reason is that if we only use our brains for mastering knowledge that already exists, we will make no contribution to the world. We will never move forward.

Improving your imagination is not as hard as it seems. It begins with curiosity – curiosity about other people, about the world around you, and about yourself.

Imagination isn't a big rainbow in the sky. It's the everyday habit of thinking, "I wonder ..."

When you develop your imagination, your brain is a much more fun place to be.

It doesn't mean ignoring facts. It means understanding facts deeply enough to know where they can lead and then going there.

The true sign of intelligence is not knowledge, but imagination.

– attributed to Albert Einstein

IMAGINE

These activities will improve your imagination very quickly:

THINK: Visualize the spelling of a word in your head. Now think of as many words as you can that begin (or even end) with the same two letters as the word you visualized.

PLAY: Games are great for building imagination, as are toys like Lego® or other building toys. Video games are less likely to help with this because they created the world for you. Create your own world.

READ: Reading invites imagination on many levels. As you read, you see in your mind the world the author describes. You predict what will come next. Your emotions stir. There are few things as good for the mind as reading.

WRITE: Fiction writing may seem more obviously imaginative than non-fiction, but even non-fiction writing involves a high level of imagination. Try writing a list of 1,000 things you like.

Tip #17
Stress Isn't Helping You, So Stop

Humans were designed to handle short-term stress with ease. The problem comes when we have long-term stress that goes on and on. This relates to that internal locus of control we talked about in Tip #7. Usually we feel stressed because we feel that things are out of our control.

Long-term stress makes you think less clearly. It increases anxiety. It undermines your ability to use your otherwise wonderful brain.

It sounds too simple to say, "just stop being stressed," but the truth is that a lot of us have very unhealthy habits that lead to a more stressful life. We can change these habits over time to decrease our stress.

> ➤ Breathe more (and more deeply). Breathe out longer than you breathe in. Pretend you are blowing out a birthday candle.

> ➤ Go outside. Spending all of our time inside isn't good for us.

> ➤ Write a list of everything that is on your mind. Get it all out.

> ➤ Exercise. Include stretching.

> ➤ Create a playlist of songs that relax you.

If you feel like the stress in your life is too much for you to handle alone, seek help from a qualified mental health professional.

For more typical stress, try this idea:

Become a Labyrinthian!

Labyrinths are excellent for reducing stress, and you can grab two sets of free printable finger labyrinths I made here:

http://bit.ly/gg-labyrinth

http://bit.ly/gg-labyrinth-2

Tip #18
Read Hard Books

I'm a big believer in reading good literature, and one of the main reasons is that hard books challenge your brain in a way little else can. Seriously, there are 559 characters in *War and Peace*.

Length and number of characters alone doesn't make a book "hard." What I mean by reading hard books is to read books that challenge your thinking. Read books that force you to consider why you think the way you do. Read books that ask you to look at things from someone else's perspective.

I promise that this isn't going to feel like a chore (at least after you get used to it). You will grow to love books that stay with you, and these are the books that do that.

Books are called "mirrors" when the characters and situations mirror our own. These are usually easy to like and understand.

Books are called "windows" when the characters and situations are different from our own lives and give us a glimpse into a different world or time or experience.

Make sure you are reading plenty of window books.

Read and Choose:

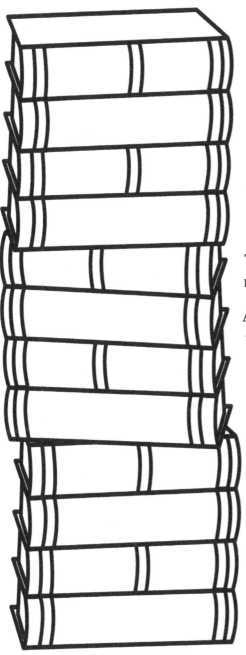

Read this article I wrote on why you should read classic literature:

http://bit.ly/read-classics.

Then choose **twelve** classics to read.

As you finish them, write their titles in the book stack to the left.

Want ideas? Try starting with *1,000 Books to Read Before You Die: A Life-Changing List* by James Mustich.

Section III:
Helpful Habits for
Gifted Brains

Tip #19
Plan Tomorrow Today

The day stretches out before you...twenty-four hours. It seems like an incredible abundance of time.

But you know what happens, don't you? Little tasks start nibbling away at that time, and by the end of the day, we've been busy without getting done what we really wanted to do.

Sometimes it feels like we're on a time roller coaster where someone else is controlling the ride. Of course, if we're kids (or have little tiny kids), that's actually true. However, sometimes the only thing in control of our time is our lack of control of our time.

What I mean is that it's up to us to tell our time what we're doing with it. If we don't, it will decide for itself, and we may not like it.

When you plan tomorrow today, you are able to hit the ground running. And it's fine if "relax with a book" is the first item on the list! This isn't about being busier. It's about being intentional with using our time.

Even if we feel like a lot of our time isn't our own to spend, when we make a list of what we're doing, we see the pockets that *are* under our control.

Planning Tomorrow Today

Planning your day doesn't have to be complicated! I like this method I made up that I call the 1-2-3 Daily Plan. How it works is that I identify the most important thing I will do that day. I write that in the top box. Then, I identify the two things I'll most benefit from doing. Sometimes those benefits are short-term, and sometimes they're long-term. Lastly, I write in three things that would be great to do. I make sure I do the top two rows before the bottom row. That makes sure the priority stays the priority.

THE MOST IMPORTANT THING I WILL DO TODAY		
TWO THINGS IT WILL BENEFIT ME MOST TO COMPLETE		
THREE THINGS THAT WOULD BE GREAT TO GET DONE		

Tip #20
Keep It Clean

I'm a big believer in the power of cleanliness and organization. Here's why: it saves time and mental energy better spent elsewhere.

If I have to spend ten minutes looking for a shoe before I leave for school, I probably feel far more stressed than is ideal. I didn't plan ten minutes to look for my shoe, so I'm late. I burned up a bunch of emotional energy, and I now I don't have it for other stuff that will come my way that day.

In addition to saving time and energy, cleanliness is a sign of gratitude. You take care of things you're thankful for. If your room is a mess, it's a sign that you don't actually value what you have enough to take care of it. Ouch.

You may tell yourself that you're just too busy, that you'd rather do other things, but it doesn't work like that. If you don't take care of your things and space with intention, they will force you to spend your time on them when you are not planning for it.

People who are messy typically spend just as much time on their stuff as neat people, it's just in random moments (like looking for a shoe), and so they don't realize it. Be intentional about the time you spend caring for your things and the space you have. It will pay off.

Cleaning Check!

1. I find myself spending time looking for things that aren't where I think they should be.

   frequently   sometimes   occasionally   never

2. I feel that my belongings are clean and organized in a way that helps me find them and use them when I need them.

   frequently   sometimes   occasionally   never

3. I feel like I probably need to be more intentional about taking care of my things on my own time, rather than when something is missing when it's needed.

   frequently   sometimes   occasionally   never

Cleanliness makes it easier to see the details.

— Aniekee Tochukwu

Tip #21
Tiny Habits = Gigantic Changes

At the beginning of the year, many people set resolutions. They set big goals to do big things. Most people never accomplish these goals.

While big, sweeping resolutions can be inspiring and wonderful, what really makes change are the tiny habits you practice every single day.

One day of hours of exercise is not as effective as twenty minutes every day. One day of binge-cleaning isn't as helpful to your daily life as five minutes a day of general pickup. Ten hours of cramming for a test is nowhere near as effective as fifteen minutes a day over a period of weeks studying the material (with quizzes!).

What really works in the long run are small habits that we practice every day, almost without thinking of them. As we get older, we naturally get more habits. It will help you enormously, almost beyond describing, if you carefully consider what small habits you could begin (just one at a time is great) that will put you on the path on which you want to be.

We are what we repeatedly do. Excellence is not an act, then, but a habit.

- Aristotle

Building Habits

There are two books I recommend about habits.

- *Atomic habits: An Easy & Proven Way to Build Good Habits & Break Bad Ones* by James Clear

- *The Power of Habit: Why We Do What We Do in Life and Business* by Charles Duhigg

(Note: Both of these are books for grown-ups, although kids can read them. There are no great books for kids on this, so if you've always wanted to write a book, here's an idea for you!)

List 5 habits you would benefit from beginning. Each habit should take no more than five minutes per day to complete.

1. _____

2. _____

3. _____

4. _____

5. _____

Tip #22
The Habit of Thanks

Get in the habit of expressing gratitude. We talked about gratitude as it relates to motivation in Tip #8. This tip relates to expressing thanks, not just feeling gratitude.

One habit that will serve you well all of your life is to express your thanks in a way that makes the person feel thanked.

Once, I bought a fairly expensive gift for someone for a wedding. I got a pre-printed note that didn't even have a signature on it that was the same one they sent to everyone. It said, "Thanks for making our day special." The irony was that they had done the opposite for me. They didn't make me feel special; they made me feel like I'd wasted my money on them. Don't be that person.

When you receive something, be the kind of person who says thank you in a way that makes the person feel thanked. There are many ways to do it (calls, texts, notes, etc.), and here's a tip: the less likely others are to do something, the more you stand out when you do.

So write a note. A real note on paper. Remember paper?

The truth is that when people express thanks well, it makes us want to give them more, so in the end, this may literally pay off. But what it's really about, though, it's about being a good person, not just a smart one.

Whom Should I Thank?

Think of three people who you could thank for things in order to build your habit of thanking people. It doesn't matter if what they gave you was a long time ago. Gratitude doesn't have an expiration date.

Want ideas? Consider people who have given you:

⮌ Good advice you ended up using

⮌ Encouragement when you were going through a hard time

⮌ Help when you were completing a project

⮌ A smile when you were having a bad day

⮌ Forgiveness when you did something that hurt them

⮌ Their time when they were busy

⮌ Suggestions when you were trying to fix something

⮌ Friendship when you were lonely

⮌ An item you needed to borrow

Tip #23
Track Your Changes

As you develop new habits or more firmly establish ones you already had, it helps to track the changes you notice. Remember dopamine and how much we love it? When we track the changes in ourselves, we get a little shot of dopamine when we see improvement.

It's important to track changes because many of them are subtle and easily missed if we don't track them.

We might not notice that the two-step, single-variable problems in Algebra class are getting easier to solve if we don't track a rating of our effort over time.

We might not notice that we went three days without having to be reminded to brush our teeth or shower or take out the trash.

My friend Andrew McBurney tracks both "Days With" and "Days Without" in order to motivate himself to better health.

Your tracking system need not be complicated. You can use an app or an index card. Just track.

Days With & Days Without

Looking for ideas? Consider tracking:

Days With:

going to bed on time

eating healthily

reading something worth reading

prayer/meditation

being kind to someone

writing in your journal

planning your day

walking 10,000 steps

exercise

posting something nice/helpful on social media

Days Without:

sugar

too much video game time

whining

contention

soda

spending money

talking too much

checking your phone too often

junk food

complaining

Tip #24

Procrastinate Only If It Serves You

Putting things off can be an art form. Some people are Olympic-level procrastinators who can put off work until the last possible nanosecond. Procrastination is not typically viewed in a positive light.

Procrastination isn't all bad, though. I have a paper tray where I put papers I want to file. I only let myself go through it every three months. Now, that may seem like procrastinating, but what really happens is that I end up recycling a lot of what's in the tray. The time between putting it in the tray and then actually filing it gives me some emotional distance from the paper. I make better decisions about what I really need to keep because I waited.

This is what some psychologists call active procrastination. I'm not procrastinating out of laziness or a lack of responsibility. I'm procrastinating in order to do a better job in the end.

Active procrastination can also protect us from things that don't really need to be done.

Passive procrastination is more common. It is the kind you're used to – that feeling you have that you just don't want to do something. That kind wastes mental energy that could be better spent elsewhere.

Active v. Passive Procrastination

For the following categories, check yourself for your level of procrastination:

Category	Active	Passive	No/very little procrastination
Work/school tasks I enjoy			
Work/school tasks I don't like			
Chores			
Returning items (to the library, to friends, etc.)			
Putting away clothes			
Returning messages or calls			
Thanking people			
Hobbies/ activities I enjoy			
Things other people ask me to do			
Things I think I should do			

Now choose two categories that you checked as passive procrastination categories and resolve to break that pattern.

Tip #25
Good Posture Is Good
For More Than Your Back

Amy Cuddy presented a TED talk on how posture can increase your personal power, and she's not alone in thinking that posture can improve your psychological health, as well as your physical health.

First, the physical. Good posture leads to better balance, fewer injuries, and stronger muscle and bone health.

Now, the brain. Good posture improves confidence. Some research shows that if you walk with good posture, you're less likely to be bullied or attacked, even by a stranger.

Posture isn't just when you're standing. When you slouch over while sitting, you inhibit air flow. Sit up straight and you can increase your oxygen intake as much as 30%. That's a lot!

When you have good posture, your chest cavity is more open, allowing more oxygen in to your body (including your brain). More oxygen in the brain equals more energy for thinking.

Better breathing also reduces stress naturally.

So sit and stand up straight!

Align your spine!

This is what the Harvard Medical School says you should do to have good posture:

When standing:

- ✓ chin parallel to the floor
- ✓ shoulders even (roll your shoulders up, back, and down to help achieve this)
- ✓ neutral spine (no flexing or arching to overemphasize the curve in your lower back)
- ✓ arms at your sides with elbows straight and even
- ✓ abdominal muscles braced
- ✓ hips even
- ✓ knees even and pointing straight ahead
- ✓ body weight distributed evenly on both feet

When sitting:

- ✓ keep your chin parallel to the floor
- ✓ shoulders, hips, and knees at even heights
- ✓ knees and feet pointing straight ahead.

Tip #26

Break Down Your Tasks to A Molecular Level

Just like having narrow goals like we talked about in Tip #2, breaking tasks down to the smallest action that matters is a habit worth developing.

One benefit is that it helps us to avoid passive procrastination (see Tip #24). It's a lot easier to tell ourselves we don't have time to clean our whole room than it is to tell ourselves we don't have time to pick up three things.

Another benefit is that it becomes easier to plan. If a task would take an hour, it's a lot harder to plan for it than if that same task were broken down into a number of five-minute micro-tasks.

Now, don't be silly and break tasks down into something so small it makes no sense (pick up pencil, put pencil on paper).

Break down the tasks into manageable bites, and you will find yourself in the habit of actually completing far more. Plus, checking off all of those tasks will give you more dopamine, and you know how I feel about that!

Break it down!

Think of a common task you have to do (homework, cleaning your room, grocery shopping, laundry, etc.). Break it down into the smallest task that matters and estimate how much time it takes to do those things.

Task: _____

Microtasks:

- _____

- _____

- _____

- _____

- _____

- _____

- _____

- _____

I long to accomplish a great and noble task, but it is my chief duty to accomplish small tasks as if they were great and noble.
- Helen Keller

Tip #27

Go Ahead and Multitask, As Long As You Don't Care About The Outcome

The research has been done, and the results are in:

It's monotasking for the win!

The idea that we can devote equal and valuable attention to the multiple tasks at the same time is a fallacy. We do both (or all) tasks less well than we would, and we don't even save time.

It turns out that what we're really doing is switching quickly from one task to the other, but it still takes the brain more time than if we fully invested ourselves in one task and then the other. When you switch between tasks, you leave a little attention with the first task, called attention residue. This slows you down mentally, and you don't have to be gifted to figure out that that's not optimal.

This is true for tasks that take the brain. You can probably walk and chew gum, as the saying says. But you can't listen and text. Two verbal processes running simultaneously in your brain is more than you can really do effectively and respectfully.

So fully invest yourself in what you're doing. Then repeat.

Prove it to yourself:

Monotask: Draw two horizontal lines on a piece of paper.

Have someone time you as you do these two things:

Write this on the first line:
>   I believe I can multitask

Write on the second line the numbers 1 – 21 in order:
>   1 2 3 4 5 6 7 8 9 10 11 12 13 14 15 16 17 18 19 20 21

What was your time? _____
(usually it's around 20 seconds)

Multitask: Draw two more horizontal lines. Have someone time you as you do these tasks:

> Write a letter on the top line, then a number on the bottom line following this pattern:
>
> > The first letter in the sentence on the top line (the one you wrote in the monotask "I believe I can multitask.")
> >
> > The first number in the sentence on the bottom line
> >
> > Then the next letter in the sentence on the top line
> >
> > Then the next number, then the next letter, and so on until you've written the entire sentence and all of the numbers from 1 – 21.
>
> So, you're writing "I" on the top line, and "1" on the bottom line. Then "b" on the top line and "2" on the bottom line, and so on.

What did you notice? Your time was surely slower, but what else did you feel going on?

Tip #28
Honor Your Working Memory Limit

No matter how smart you are, your working memory has limits. Your working memory is what you use in mental tasks like language comprehension (holding onto ideas early in a sentence to use later), problem solving (holding the number from the ones column to the tens column), and even planning ("I'm going to turn in my paper, then pack up my backpack, and then check to see if my mom texted me.").

This has limits, and you can overtax it with distraction. You will do better in class if you save your working memory space for what is actually going on in class rather than thinking about what you'll do after class. The same is true for meetings and other situations.

Don't use up your storage holding irrelevant information.

Some people have better, stronger working memories than others, but for everyone there is a limit. Honor that limit by only asking your working memory to invest itself in what is really important right now.

Don't waste your precious brain resources on unrelated, unnecessary mental tasks.

Think of three activities you do that challenge your working memory: (such as paying attention in class, reading, and playing games):

1. _____

2. _____

3. _____

Now list things that you sometimes think about that may be using up your working memory while you are doing those things:

1. _____

2. _____

3. _____

4. _____

5. _____

The next time you are doing one of the three activities you listed, be conscious of thoughts that may be interfering with your working memory.

Tip #29
Be Honest With Yourself About Self-Distraction

Lots of people believe they study better when they listen to music. Lots of people are wrong.

As we learned in Tip #27, multitasking isn't all it's cracked up to be, and listening to music is a type of distraction.

While you can find lists of positive things about listening to music, those things have not really been studied in the context of distraction. Yes, music reduces stress and has other great benefits, but if you listen to music with lyrics while reading or writing (and that includes doing math), you tend to be less efficient and have lower comprehension.

Lots of times we think we're listening to music while we study, but we really tune it out in order to concentrate, only noticing when a line from a favorite song comes on.

Music isn't the only distractor. We use our phones to distract us (see Tip #12), and we often distract ourselves from necessary tasks with less important ones.

If you've got an efficient brain, don't be your own worst enemy by inviting distraction. Shun it and focus.

Distraction Action

Here's a list of common distractions while we're working or studying. Look through the list. If any affect you, write on the line next to it what you could do to minimize that distraction (e.g., "noise-cancelling headphones," "move to a different location").

noise   _____

smartphones _____

clutter   _____

interruptions _____

hunger   _____

social media _____

Other   _____

Section IV:

Out of Giftedland

And into The World

Tip #30
Stop Complaining

When you have a proficient brain, you can't help but notice how things could be done, well, better. You'll notice inefficiencies, a lack of optimization of resources, and other issues that seem glaringly obvious and very easy to fix. And yet, people don't fix them. It's incredibly annoying.

When this happens, the tendency is often to express this annoyance vocally. Very vocally. To anyone who will listen. Maybe if we complain loudly enough or to the right person, someone will fix it. Maybe we can get the whole world running better! It'll be so great!

Unfortunately, it doesn't work like that. What really happens is that the people we are complaining to aren't usually the ones who can actually help. Usually they're the ones willing to listen.

We can wear out even our closest and best friends and most loving family members with our constant complaining. And this is true even if we don't recognize it as complaining. Even if to us it seems to be just an acknowledgement of how badly something is being done and how easily it could be made better. Friends, that's called complaining.

Even when you're right (and you often are), it's a downer for those around you. It's an emotional drain they don't deserve.

So stop.

Complaining Quiz

Do you complain too much? Let's find out!

Circle AGREE or DISAGREE with the following statements:

1. When I notice something that could be done better, I frequently share my observations with others, even if they're not the ones in charge.

AGREE   DISAGREE

2. Most of my close friends or family members could easily come up with four or five things I frequently complain about.

AGREE   DISAGREE

3. I am more likely to comment on something when it's *not* going well than when it *is* going well.

AGREE   DISAGREE

4. If something isn't being done well, it's helpful if someone points out how it could be done better. How else will it improve?

AGREE   DISAGREE

I think you can figure out how this is scored. If you agree with more than two of these, you may want to reevaluate your level of complaining.

Tip #31
Sometimes It Hurts To Ask

Ever heard the saying, "It can't hurt to ask"? It's not true.

Sometimes it can hurt to ask. Consider that the ask itself is a favor. You are putting someone in the position of having to decide if they are going to do or give what you are asking for.

If they give it to you, it may inconvenience them or cost them something they needed or wanted. If they don't give it to you, they have to figure out a way to tell you they're not going to give it to you.

Both of these responses have a cost. We can wear people out asking, even if in our minds we're thinking, "Well, if she doesn't want to, she can just say no."

It's not that easy. Saying "no" uses up emotional energy, as well as time. When we turn someone down, we almost always feel badly at some level, even if that level is just annoyance.

Sometimes we don't realize what we're asking. We don't think about what the real implications are, or what the ask will feel like to the person.

Consider carefully how often you ask for favors or make requests.

Asked & Answered

Think of a time someone asked you for something and it made you feel uncomfortable or you wished they hadn't asked for it.

_____

_____

_____

_____

Think of the most common things you ask for & of whom you ask them. What is one thing you could do to make your asking more respectful of their time and mental energy?

_____

_____

_____

_____

Tip #32
Practice Situational Awareness

In the military, there is a term called *situational awareness* that is used pretty frequently. You can find a lot of definitions for it, but essentially it means:

➲ You have an accurate perception of what's going on around you.

➲ You understand what those things mean.

➲ You make an accurate guess of what's going to happen in the near future based on your perception and understanding.

Sometimes, very smart people have little or no situational awareness. They are clueless about what's going on around them in a way that makes them seem like they don't care about anyone but themselves. That's not very smart.

This can be temporary, like when you're in the middle of a great book, and you forget what planet you're on. It can also be more permanent, almost a way of being that can come across as arrogant and clueless.

Probably "arrogant" and "clueless" aren't words you'd like to hear used to describe you. I'm just guessing here.

Practicing situational awareness, just being *aware* of situational awareness, will help you function more optimally in a way that is likely to lead to better outcomes than obliviousness to the world around you.

Lack of Awareness Assessment

There are times we're more likely to have a lack of situational awareness than other times. If we're deeply concentrating on studying or work, it's normal to tune out the world. It's worth thinking about if there are times, though, when we would benefit from more situational awareness.

Circle the items on this list that match times you may have less situational awareness than is optimal.

When you are:

reading

eating

driving

playing video games

playing something other than a video game

on your phone

Tip #33
Adjust Your Sails

When I was younger growing up in California, we had a small sailboat named *Spirit*. While my mom was the real sailor in the family, I did learn some techniques. One critical aspect of sailing is trimming the sails. Good sail trim is a result of reading the wind and adjusting to it to keep the sail's shape optimal. This keeps the boat in balance and makes it sail as efficiently as possible.

To help sailors read the wind, there are pieces of cloth called *telltales* that are sewn on different points of the sail to help you know if your sail is trimmed optimally. Based on what you see, you will need to adjust your sails.

You have telltales in your life that will let you know if you need to adjust your sails. While everyone's telltales are different, we all have indicators that we need adjustment.

Trimming your sails may mean spending more or less time on an activity, or more or less time with a person. It may mean adjusting as simple as the volume of your voice. There are thousands of possible adjustments we can make to be more in balance.

Learning to read your telltales and adjust your sails will benefit you all of your life, so practice as often as you can.

Do you need to trim your sails?

Trimming the sails is all about the sails' relationship to the wind. As the wind changes, the trim needs to change as well. In our lives, we may be doing just fine until our situation changes. If we don't recognize that we need to trim our sails, we will end up in trouble, or at least not as well off as we otherwise would be if we'd paid more attention to the telltales.

What are your telltales that help you know when you need to trim your sails? Do you have friends or family who help you? Do you have a journal that reveals your changing patterns? Do you have a gut feeling?

Write down clues you can or should watch for to tell if you need to make adjustments.

Tip #34
Have Reasonable Expectations

When you have unreasonable expectation of things, events or people, you will be less happy. It's been said by many people that expectations are resentments in the making, and this is true.

Now, it's impossible not to have any expectations, obviously. What is optimal is to have reasonable expectations. When you go to school, it would be optimal if the teacher is gifted, all the kids in the class are gifted, there's no standardized testing, and you can work at your own pace. I'll wait for a second while you wake up from that dream.

What's reasonable is different from what's optimal.

When we have reasonable expectations, we make it less likely that we'll walk around feeling resentful.

We have to make sure that the expectations we have are reasonable to the people and things we're interacting with, not just to us. For instance, it may seem reasonable to you that if a conversation is boring, you should just end it, saying, "This is boring." Other people will have different expectations of how the conversation will end.

The alternate reality in which everything is exactly as you think it should be exists only in your mind, and it exists primarily to torture you.

- Cheri Huber

Expectation Check-in

Think about some of the expectations you have and rate them on how reasonable you think they are. Be honest with yourself about the reasonableness!

Check the box under "yes" or "no" to indicate if you think your expectations in the areas below are reasonable. There are three blank boxes for you to fill in with other areas of your life not included for which you have expectations.

Area of Expectation	Yes	No
friendships		
amount of free time I should have		
how other people will treat me		
how often my friends will call/text/message me		
how much feedback I'll get on my work		
how much time I should spend on my work		
work/school in general		

For any expectations that you indicated "no," consider what you could do to adjust those expectations, even just a little.

Tip #35
Learn To Self-Sooth In Boredom

If I lift heavy weights, I will feel it the next day. My son who is in the U.S. Army has to lift much heavier weights in order to notice the effort. While the brain is more complicated than muscle, the principle is the same: your brain needs a challenge if it's going to grow.

Sometimes it's hard for a gifted brain to find challenge in places that we'd expect (like school).

If we don't feel sufficiently challenged, we often call that boredom. You don't need to accept feeling bored. Recognize it, and then fix it.

Part of what it means to be smart is to be an active owner of your brain. It's important to figure out how to challenge yourself.

You can create problems in your head, think of ways that what you're doing could be made more challenging, connect what you're hearing or seeing with other knowledge you have, and on and on. The possibilities for what your brain can do are almost unlimited. Even just thinking, "This is uncomfortable, but I can tolerate it" is better than letting yourself get all worked up.

Avoid being one of those people who always needs someone else to task their brain. Task your own brain. Boredom can lead to creativity instead of frustration if you take charge.

Test yourself on the Boredom Proneness Scale, developed by researchers at the University of Oregon, by visiting gotoquiz.com/boredom_proness_scale.

What did you find out? Do you agree with the results? Did anything surprise you?

_____

_____

_____

_____

What is one strategy you can use when you're feeling bored?

_____

And if you're really interested in boredom (that sounds weird), there's a great book called *Boredom: A Lively History* by Peter Toohey that's worth a read.

Tip #36
Patience, Young Grasshopper

In the 1970s, there was a TV show called "Kung Fu" about a half-American, half-Chinese man. The show was a western, and the character had been trained as a Shaolin monk in China who was now roaming the wild west looking for his brother, armed with only his martial arts skills and his monk training. I know; it's an interesting premise for a show.

In flashbacks, the character would remember his training master, who called him "Grasshopper." Now if you're ever on *Jeopardy!,* you'll know where the saying, "Patience, young Grasshopper" came from.

I use this long introduction to illustrate a point: you need to develop patience. You had to be patient just to figure out what I meant by the title. Patience is worth developing as a skill, especially because the gifted aren't usually famous for it.

Our impatience often manifests itself in annoyance and irritation. Newsflash: These qualities don't make us popular or easy to get along with.

If you need to develop more patience, know that it can be done. As you develop more patience, you will be happier because you will have fewer feelings of annoyance and irritation. And that's a good thing, young Grasshopper.

Creating a Patience Plan

We can developing patience in three separate areas:

1.   **Interpersonal**: patience with other people

2.   **Hardships**: patience with setbacks or obstacles

3.   **Daily Hassles**: patience with the little things like delays or things not working quite right that happen every day

Which of the three areas is your greatest challenge?

_____

Here are tips for developing patience. Look them over and choose one or two to try.

1. Understand that we can get addicted to annoyance & anger. It's a holdover from our reptilian brains. One tip is to consciously recognize that fact in the moment and reject it.

2. Use self-talk to tell yourself a different story than the one the impatience is telling you. For example, this one setback is probably not going to ruin your life forever. Be mindful of the story you're telling yourself & evaluate if it's helping or hurting.

3. Practice making yourself wait, even when you don't have to.

4. Keep track of times you get impatient (just use tally marks – it doesn't have to be complicated). Track your progress over time.

5. Make a list of the things/people that/who most often lead to feelings of impatience and plan ahead for dealing with them.

Tip #37
Self-Regulate

When I was a high school assistant principal, I had a sign on the wall in my office next to the chair where students sat that said: "You can either be a good example or a terrible warning."

Virtually every student who ended up in my office was there because he or she had not controlled himself or herself. They then had to have me control them. If I couldn't control them with discussion, detention, or even suspension, then they would end up at our special school where they had no choices and everything was controlled for them.

People would ask me, "How do you make kids be good?" I would answer, "I can't make them act appropriately, but I can make them wish they had."

Deciding to be a good example rather than a terrible warning is basically what self-regulation is. It's owning the idea that the best person to be in charge of you *is* you, and knowing that if you don't control yourself, others will control you.

If taken to the extreme, a lack of self-regulation can land you in prison, where you no longer have control over your environment.

Self-regulate. It's the habit of the truly wise. Don't let your emotions overwhelm your intelligence.

Self-Regulation Self-Check

In Dan Goleman's books on emotional intelligence, he identifies self-regulation as one of five core components of an emotionally intelligent person. He defines it as, "managing one's internal states, impulses, and resources." He breaks it down into five competencies you can develop:

- **Self-control**: keeping disruptive emotions and impulses in check

- **Trustworthiness**: maintaining standards of honesty and integrity

- **Conscientiousness**: taking responsibility for personal performance

- **Adaptability**: flexibility in handling change

- **Innovation**: being comfortable with novel ideas, approaches, and new information

Put a star next to the one you think you're best at.

Underline the one you think you need to develop that would help you the most.

On a scale of 1 – 10,

how strong is your self-regulation? ____

Section V:

Soft Skills, Firm Results

Tip #38
Mindfulness Is Pure Power

Pay attention and be fully present in the moment without judgment. That's mindfulness.

The reason I say it's pure power is because people there is simply no greater power than to be fully in control of your own mind. When you develop habits of mindfulness, you can have:

- ✓ lower anxiety (possibly because you're not worrying about what's coming up next; you're just focused on what's right now)

- ✓ increased attention and focus

- ✓ more feelings of calmness

- ✓ a stronger sense of feeling connected to the task or activity you're doing and the people with whom you are involved

- ✓ higher awareness of what's going on around you (remember situational awareness from Tip #32?)

- ✓ increased thinking clarity

The list goes on and on, but these are the benefits I think are most important to the gifted.

When you decide that you will focus on what is happening to you right here, right now, and set aside what is not, great things happen.

Mindful, not Mindful

For each of the scenarios below, circle whether your behavior in those situations is typically either "mindful" or "not mindful."

➲ at school or work when someone else is talking

MINDFUL   NOT MINDFUL

➲ doing chores

MINDFUL   NOT MINDFUL

➲ while driving (or being a passenger)

MINDFUL   NOT MINDFUL

➲ when reading directions

MINDFUL   NOT MINDFUL

➲ in a conversation with friends

MINDFUL   NOT MINDFUL

Get a list of mindfulness activities developed by my best friend, Patricia Bear, who's a therapist, at
http://bit.ly/bear-mindfulness.

Tip #39
Kindness Is Selfish

It may seem like kindness is a favor you do the world, but in actuality, it's a favor you do yourself that benefits the world.

Here are some of the benefits you derive from being kind:

- ✓ Increased levels of serotonin, a neurotransmitter associated with feelings of well-being and satisfaction.
- ✓ Increase in what is called "positive affect" – that's how often you feel positive things like joy, alertness and interest in what you're doing. People with low levels of positive affect tend to have higher levels of social anxiety, so kindness may help you lower that, as well.
- ✓ You may live longer. If you're kind, you're more likely to have a strong social circle. People with strong social circles have lowered rates of heart disease. So kindness is actually good for your heart!
- ✓ "Helper's High" is the feeling you get when you help someone else. It activates the pleasure and reward center in the brain.
- ✓ Decreased sense of pain because of higher levels of endorphins.
- ✓ Less cortisol (a stress hormone) means lower levels of stress. This is in people who are typically kind, not just kind one day to someone they like.

There are even more benefits than these, but the message is clear: kindness is good for everyone, not just the beneficiary of the kindness.

Here's an acrostic of the word KINDNESS. Next to each letter, write something you could do to show kindness (in general or to someone specifically) that begins with that letter.

K   _____

I   _____

N   _____

D   _____

N   _____

E   _____

S   _____

S   _____

No act of kindness, no matter how small, is ever wasted.

- Aesop

Tip #40
Learn How To Learn Names

Every viewer cringed when the character Ross from the TV show *Friends*, married a girl named Emily. Why? Because at the crucial moment he said "I take thee, Rachel," calling Emily by the name of his former love interest. Oops.

When you remember people's names, you demonstrate to them that you think they are important.

Our names are important to us, and we have trouble trusting people who don't take the time to learn them if we think they should.

You may have had the experience of being called by the wrong name before, and it's not something that makes you feel really good inside.

Note: This isn't the same as when your mom calls you by your brother's name. That's called "misnaming" and it's related to a neurological experience called "spreading activation." It's not her fault, and it doesn't mean she doesn't love you.

Make it a point to learn people's names and call them by their names.

My friend Sherry Neaves is a high school teacher who makes a point to learn her students' names within the first three weeks of school to show them how important they are to her. It's no coincidence that they love her.

Hacks for Learning Names

➲ The most effective way to remember someone's name is to actually **pay attention** when they tell it to you or someone introduces you. Bonus points if you repeat it ("Nice to meet you, Severus").

➲ Think of how the person **reminds you** of another person you know. If you meet Lily and you think about how she reminds you of Hermione, you have one more neural pathway that leads to Lily's name. Just don't call her Hermione.

➲ Find **something unique** about the person. If you notice when you meet Ron that he has a really big nose or really red hair, you add to the remarkableness of the person, making it more likely you'll remember him/her.

➲ Make sure you can **spell it**. The brain doesn't usually care to remember things it thinks are nonsense. If there's a name that you don't know how to spell, you're less likely to be able to spell it. Check on spelling if you're unsure.

Tip #41
You Can't Die On Every Hill

In the military, there's a saying of unknown origin that indicates whether a certain mission is worthwhile: "That's a hill worth dying for." You'll also hear, "That's not a hill worth dying on."

In non-military life, there are hills that are metaphorically not worth dying for. The math is clear: even if you're a cat with nine lives, you can't die on every hill.

What that means is that you have to accept that some things aren't worth fighting for. Some things you just have to let go.

I hate even typing that, to be honest, because I have the emotional energy to fight every single battle. The truth is, however, that most people don't, and part of functioning optimally is not just doing what works for *us*, but what works *best*.

You've likely heard the correlated saying, "You have to pick your battles." That's what this means. Even if something seems wrong, sometimes you have to just let it be wrong.

This is one of the most difficult things for a gifted mind. It plays to our intensities. It is when our tenaciousness goes haywire. If you can learn to balance it, you will be happier and more successful in achieving your goals.

Picking the Right Hill to Fight On

Trying to decide if it's the right hill to die on? Ask yourself:

- ⊙ Will this be important to me in six months?

- ⊙ Is this the right time to bring this up?

- ⊙ Do others care much more or much less about this than I do?

- ⊙ Will lasting harm be done if this isn't addressed?

- ⊙ Is this my battle, or is it really someone else's? Sometimes we need to fight others' battles, but that's not as common as we like to think it is.

- ⊙ If I lose this battle, will more harm be done than if I had never fought it?

Tip #42
Practice the Art Of The Apology

The Joker doesn't like apologies. In fact, he says he hates them more than he hates anything. You have to admit that with the Joker, that's a high bar.

If the Joker hates something, odds are that good people like it. This is true of apologies.

The ability to make a good apology is a skill everyone needs, and since gifted people tend to offend people frequently (because of strong verbal skills combined with a penchant for sarcasm), it's a skill you need.

You may have heard people say, "Sorry, not sorry" when they don't care if their behavior is a problem or if they know they're behavior is upsetting, but they're fine with that.

Don't be that person.

Be a person who recognizes when an apology is warranted and offers a sincere apology without prompting. Only two-year-olds should have to be told, "Say 'sorry'."

A quality apology is a sign of maturity and integrity.

Keep in mind...

When you're offering an apology, keep these things in mind if you want to be a quality apologizer.

⮑ You may need to ask if you can apologize. Sometimes people aren't ready to hear it yet.

⮑ Leave out the "if." As soon as you say, "if" as in "I'm sorry if I hurt you," you have just demonstrated that you are not actually giving an apology. You're passive aggressively telling the person no reasonable person would have been hurt by what you did or said.

⮑ Make sure there's a promise in there. You need to promise not to do the same thing again, otherwise it's not really an apology. There's a saying, "The only true apology is changed behavior," and that's true in many cases. Make sure you intend to change your behavior.

⮑ Specifically ask for forgiveness. When you say, "Will you please forgive me," you send two messages. First, you're signaling that you realize forgiveness is needed, making your apology more sincere. Secondly, you're giving the incident closure. If someone agrees to forgive you, but still holds a grudge, that's on them, not you.

Tip #43
Practice 3-Step Praise

There's an old TV show called *Leave it to Beaver* that had one of the most annoying characters ever to grace the screen. His name was Eddie Haskell, and he was the kind of person who always acted sweet, but was really trouble with a capital T.

In one episode of the show, he offers this praise to his friend's mom:

Eddie: Gee, your kitchen always looks so clean.

June Cleaver: Why, thank you, Eddie.

Eddie: My mother says it looks as though you never do any work in here.

Um. Thanks?

When you give praise there are three steps to making it effective and meaningful.

1. Say the person's name.

2. Say specifically what they did, not just some general, breezy "thanks!"

3. Explain what positive effect their actions had on you or someone else.

Follow this pattern, and you'll never be like Eddie Haskell. I hope.

Who Deserves Praise from You?

Think of people (or even a group of some kind) to whom you could offer genuine praise. Fill in the chart below identifying not only who they are, but also specifically what they did and what effect it had on you or someone else. Then, offer that praise.

Name of Person	What did they do?	What effect did it have?

Tip #44
Empathy Trumps Sympathy

The Greek root *pathos* means "feeling" or "suffering." It's where we get the word *sympathy*, meaning "to feel with" or "affected by like feelings."

Empathy is actually a newer word in the English language (It's only about 100 years old). It is intended to mean something deeper than sympathy.

Empathy means that not only do you feel badly for something, but you can actually put yourself in his or her shoes and imagine or feel what it is like to be feeling what he or she is feeling.

Actor Jared Leto said, "I've always liked Saturn. But I also have some sympathy for Pluto because I heard it's been downgraded from a planet, and I think it should remain a planet. Once you've given something planetary status it's kind of mean to take it away."

Jared can't have empathy for Pluto because he's never been granted planetary status, but he can have sympathy.

When you feel empathy for someone, you are better able to comfort that person. You're less likely to say something hurtful. Use that gifted brain to really try to imagine what it's like to be in the situation.

It might be painful to do so, but usually our friends are worth it when it means we can be better friends to them.

Sympathy v. Empathy

You're not always able or expected to empathize. Sometimes sympathy is enough. You may not be able to understand what someone's situation is. When it is possible, however, it's a more helpful way to be. Here's what the difference looks like in practical ways.

Sympathy	Empathy
You feel sorry for someone.	You understand how they feel.
You **think** that what the person is going through would be hard.	You **know** that what the person is going through is hard.
You **say** you're sorry.	You **show** that you're sorry by doing something for them or with them.
You say, "Let me know if there's anything I can do."	You ask, "Can I do this (something you think might help) for you?"
You remember that they are going through a hard time.	You remember that they are going through a hard time, and you keep reaching out.

Tip #45

Every Environment Has Its Own Emotional Ecosystem

When my son Jonathan was in elementary school, one day he said to me, "The cafeteria is my most difficult society."

He recognized a truth about social situations: every environment has its own emotional ecosystem. Even school has different emotional ecosystems. The locker room is different from the classroom, and the classroom is different from the principal's office.

Emotional ecology is a lot like an environmental ecosystem. Different species survive and thrive in different ecosystems.

Similarly, different people survive and thrive in different emotional ecosystems. The same person who gets along really well with people in one situation, may crash and burn socially in another situation.

Try to become adept at understanding what the emotional ecosystem you're in is demanding of you and decide if you want to develop the skills it's asking for. The answer may be "no," and that's fine. The important thing is to recognize the difference and make a decision, rather than just wondering why you are struggling socially in an environment.

What are your emotional ecosystems?

Identify three emotional ecosystems in which you function (school/work, church, and home, for example).

Label each oval in the Venn diagram below with an ecosystem and identify one or two traits necessary or helpful in that ecosystem. Then, identify traits that are helpful in multiple venues in the overlapping areas of the diagram.

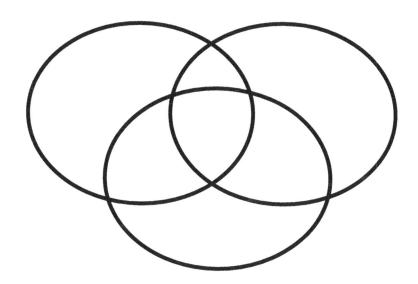

Section VI:

Mentor Your Mind

Tip #46
Inventory Your Strengths Honestly

Once, I had a boss who, when asked about her strengths, said, "Oh! Interpersonal skills, for sure!" There was dead silence in the room, as all of us who worked for her thought, "Um, no. That is absolutely not true."

Sometimes what we think of as our strengths are not. The same is true of weaknesses, of course, but I'm talking about strengths because people focus so often on them in the gifted population.

It's important to be honest about our strengths for two reasons:

- We are allowed to have strengths, even though people sometimes try to make us feel arrogant just for acknowledging that we have strengths. If we don't recognize our own strengths, it will be harder for us to acknowledge and celebrate strengths in others.

- We don't always have strengths in areas typical of the gifted. If we just assume that we have strong verbal skills because that's common in the gifted population, we can end up frustrated with ourselves unnecessarily. By being honest about our strengths, we can be more patient with ourselves in other areas.

Your Strengths

On the left, list things you feel are strengths. On the right, list things that people sometimes assume you have a strength in, when really you are not necessarily stronger than normal in that area.

Strengths I Have

Strengths People Assume I Have

_____   _____

_____   _____

_____   _____

_____   _____

_____   _____

Few men during their lifetime come anywhere near exhausting the resources dwelling within them. There are deep wells of strength that are never used.

—Richard E. Byrd

Tip #47
Invest In One Development Opportunity Every Week

Shane Parrish is a Canadian former spy who turned his intelligence analysis skills into a website and podcast where he shares ideas on how to think more effectively. Every week, I get his newsletter that shares articles worth reading, book recommendations and other ideas that fit his message: Upgrade Yourself.

It's important to set aside time to grow in ways you choose, not just ways that are chosen for you. I have to learn things for my work. That doesn't mean that that's all I need in order to grow in ways that are important to me.

You probably have things you have to learn for school or work, and it's easy to think that those things are enough. They're not. You need to invest in your own growth and learning yourself.

One opportunity per week is a good place to start. Come up with one thing you will do each week to grow and learn. It doesn't need to be different each week, and it also doesn't need to be the same.

If you'd like to get Shane's newsletter, too, you can subscribe to it at https://fs.blog/newsletter.

Opportunities to Develop Yourself

✓ Read quality Books or articles.

✓ Learn another language (see Tip #13).

✓ Write on a blog or work on writing a book.

✓ Take an online course.

✓ Practice an instrument or take a lesson.

✓ Learn to cook something.

✓ Learn or practice an athletic skill or game.

✓ Learn or practice a hobby where you create something (carpentry, knitting, etc.).

✓ Go to the library and see how much you can learn in an hour.

Tip #48
Create Measurable Benchmarks

A number of years ago, I had a goal I set for myself as a New Year's Resolution: I wanted to increase my kindness (see Tip #39). As the months went by, I struggled to figure out if it was working. Was I more kind? How would I know? I would ask people, "Am I kinder than I used to be?" They'd look at me strangely, as you can imagine.

Here's the problem: I had no way to measure it and no way to check in with myself with any kind of objectivity.

I ended up taking a composition notebook and calling it my "Kindness Notebook." Every day, I'd write down anything I'd done that showed kindness to others. I made a list of kindness ideas in the back of the notebook, and I began taking time once a month to look over what I'd done and give myself a kindness grade.

When you're trying to get better at something, make sure that you figure out a way to measure it, and make sure you set specific times to check in.

If you don't, you'll end up like me asking random strangers how nice you are.

Well, it probably won't get that bad, but you see what I mean.

Goals & Benchmarks

Think of some goals you have for yourself and list them in the left-hand column of the chart below. In the middle column, explain how you measure your progress, and in the right-hand column explain how often you check in with your overall progress.

Goal	How I Measure It	Benchmark

Our ambition should be to rule ourselves, the true kingdom for each one of us; and true progress is to know more, and be more, and to do more.

– Oscar Wilde

Tip #49
Track Your Progress Like A Scientist

A.J. Jacobs has become a bestselling author by making himself a human guinea pig and then writing about it. He wrote *The Know-It-All* about trying to learn everything in the world. He wrote *The Year of Living Biblically* about trying to keep all of the commandments and rules in the Bible exactly. He wrote *Drop Dead Healthy*...well, you can see what he does.

He decides to do something, and he documents it while he does it. Then he makes it into something other people pay money to read.

He has done this by keeping track.

Scientists keep track of their results. When they conduct experiments, they keep meticulous data on what happened.

Tracking your progress on your endeavors in the same way a scientist would makes it more likely you will succeed. It has another advantage as well: it gives you some emotional distance from the thing you're working on. That's useful because it helps to prevent discouragement. Over time, you see the way the data moves up and down, and you can grasp the arc of the change, rather than feeling defeated by a single failed attempt.

Calling it an experiment gives you permission to fail.
– A.J. Jacobs

Tracking Tools

To track your progress like a scientist, you'll need a place to track. There are many options, and the best one is the one you will actually use. If you start tracking and find that it isn't working, switch to a different one.

Here are some possibilities:

- Journal (traditional or bullet journal)

- White board

- Spreadsheet

- Sticker chart

- App (there are dozens, so browse around)

- Don't Break the Chain (a calendar where you put an "x" every day you engage in the desired behavior and you try not to break the chain of them)

Tip #50
Get 360° Feedback

In business it's a fairly common practice in some large companies now to have something called a 360° review. This is where feedback on the person's performance is solicited from the boss, the colleagues, and the people the person manages, if there are any. It can be really horrible, because it's anonymous, so people can say anything they want, whether it's accurate or helpful. It's sometimes very hurtful.

So why am I suggesting it?

I'm not suggesting that you get that kind of 360° review. I'm suggesting that you make a point to gather feedback from people other than just the ones who evaluate your work. So if you're a student, get feedback from people other than just the teacher. Ask other students what they think. Get feedback from your family.

Tell people clearly what kind of feedback you're seeking. If you only want praise, tell them that, although I would argue that's a waste of time. If you really want to improve, consider getting feedback that leads to improvement.

When you do this, you take back power over your work. It's not just a single boss or teacher who evaluates your efforts. This is key when you are actually trying to improve, not simply complete an assignment.

The value of the feedback you get depends upon three things:

1. The honesty and skill of the person you ask.

2. The clarity with which you asked for the kind of feedback you want.

3. Your willingness to hear the feedback without becoming defensive.

Here are a few questions you can use to get feedback:

- "I'm hoping to do this even better/more effectively next time. What's something you think I could do to improve it?"

- "If you could change one thing about this to make it better, what would you change?"

- "Do you think this was the optimal presentation style/color/font/material for this project?"

- "To me, the greatest strength of this is ____, and it's greatest weakness is ____. What do you think is the greatest strength and greatest weakness?"

- "I'm looking for three things I could do differently next time. I have one. Do you have one you could add?"

Tip #51
Curate A Canon

Ben Sasse is a professor and senator from Nebraska who believes in reading in a big way. In one of his books, he wrote about creating a "family canon" of sixty books. He says, "I do strongly believe that every American family should be developing their own canon of books they read together and repeatedly — and moreover that we should be comparing our lists with those of our neighbors and fellow citizens, so that we might enrich one another."

The word "canon" is from a Greek root meaning "standard" or "measuring rod." A canon of books is a set of books that are considered to be the most important or influential.

If you are to grow your mind, you must grow your library. That library must be filled with books that are of lasting value to you. I'm not saying you can't read just for fun – of course you can! I'm saying that you should also read to grow as a human, to gain insight into the thoughts of others, to consider the ideas of great minds, and to challenge your own thoughts.

Your canon will change over time, and that's fine.

What's important is to have a set of books you rely on to fuel deep, meaningful thinking.

How to Build a Canon

There are dozens of lists of great books that you can use to inspire your choices, yet I would suggest that you select books that are meaningful to you. Don't add a book to the canon that you haven't read yet.

Use a variety of types of books: fiction, non-fiction, philosophy, history, art, etc.

Make a separate space on the shelves for the canon, so it's special.

If you'd like a little more inspiration, you can read an interview with Ben Sasse at http://bit.ly/sasse-reads.

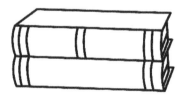

Tip #52
Listen and Learn

When I was a teenager, my mom won a big speech contest with a speech about listening. In the speech, she quoted this old English nursery rhyme:

A wise old owl lived in an oak
The more he saw the less he spoke
The less he spoke the more he heard.
Why can't we all be like that wise old bird?

Gifted individuals are often great talkers. I've gotten in serious trouble in school for talking too much, even when I was the teacher!

What we're sometimes not as good at is listening. Listening is more than waiting for your turn to talk.

Listening is interesting because it actually makes you a better talker, even though talking doesn't necessarily make you a better listener.

When you practice listening, you demonstrate respect for others' opinions and ideas. You learn more, enriching your own opinions. You make it more likely that people will listen to your thoughts, too.

Learning to be a better listener is key to becoming a better thinker.

Listening Tips

Here are some practices and habits that can help you develop your listening skills:

- ✓ Maintain eye contact. If that's super uncomfortable for you, make sure you are glancing at the person's eyes frequently. Listening is an eye exercise as much as it is an ear exercise.

- ✓ Put away your phone. If you're looking at a screen while someone is talking, that is not listening.

- ✓ If you need a challenge to keep yourself engaged, practice thinking about what the person is *not* saying. What is he/she leaving out?

- ✓ Leave a little pause after the person finishes before you jump in with your own thoughts. That way, you signal that you were really listening, not just impatiently waiting for your turn.

BONUS TIP
Embrace The Cautionary Tale

A cautionary tale is a folk tale that has a goal: warn the reader of danger. Cautionary tales are told in three parts, and they follow in a certain order. First, something has to be identified as being dangerous. Next, the story is told. In the story, someone ignores the warning about danger and does the dangerous thing. Lastly, bad things happen to that person. In older folk tales, it gets pretty grisly.

You can probably think of fairy tales you've read that are cautionary tales designed to help you not break in to people's houses *(Little Red Riding Hood),* not be greedy (*King Midas*), not to lie (*The Boy Who Cried Wolf*), and more.

If you pay attention, you will hear lots of cautionary tales that are far less formal than folk and fairy tales, but no less important.

Watch for what happens to people around you. Learn to learn from the choices and consequences of others. Be a person who doesn't have to touch the stove to know it's hot. Be a person who can watch someone else and learn from their successes and mistakes.

When you can see what someone else has done and evaluate if that is a good choice for you or not, you are on a path to wisdom.

My Cautionary Tale

Think of an experience you've had that could
benefit someone else.

Have you learned something through painful experience? Have
you had something wonderful happen because of a good choice?

In the space below, share your story.

_____

_____

_____

_____

_____

_____

About the Author

Using a combination of neuropsychology, pedagogy, experience, humor, technology and sheer fun, Lisa Van Gemert shares best practices in gifted education with audiences around the world.

She is an expert consult to television shows including Lifetime's "Child Genius," and a writer of award-winning lesson plans, as well as numerous published articles on social psychology and pedagogy and the Legacy Award-winning book, *Perfectionism: A Practical Guide to Managing Never Good Enough*.

A former teacher, school administrator, and Youth & Education Ambassador for Mensa, she shares resources for educators and parents on her website GiftedGuru.com. Lisa and her Aussie husband Steve are the parents of lots of sons (one is in the picture with her) and live in Arlington, Texas.

Lisa loves hearing from readers, so please email her at lisa@giftedguru.com and join the conversation on her website or Facebook page https://www.facebook.com/GiftedGuru.

About the Artist

Dan Darr is an artist whose murals can be found in homes all around the Dallas-Fort Worth area and whose artwork has won major awards in juried shows. Dan graduated from Texas A&M University with a degree in Environmental Design and he currently teaches art at Martin High School.

Years ago, Dan dated one of Lisa's friends, Susan, and when they were getting married, they entered a radio station contest to win the wedding of their dreams. Lisa leveraged the school district email to rally teachers to vote for them (they won!), and a lasting friendship was forged.

Later, they all worked together at Martin High School where Lisa fell in love with Dan's art, especially his satirical works about high school shenanigans (which she still owns originals of!).

When it was time for this book, Lisa knew there was only one person to design the cover, and that was Dan. She commissioned the globe brain, and his wife Susan suggested the primary colors for the continents, so it was truly a team effort.

Dan is also a talented musician who plays drums in a jazz trio, Three if by Sea, and he lives in Arlington with his wife Susan, their three kids, and their super nice dog Daisy.

If you would like to get in touch with Dan or would like to learn more about his art, visit: dannydarr.com

Made in the USA
Monee, IL
13 August 2021

75526761R10075